Snapshot Americana

Snapshot Americana

Jeff Musillo

Winchester, UK
Washington, USA

First published by Roundfire Books, 2014
Roundfire Books is an imprint of John Hunt Publishing Ltd., Laurel House, Station Approach,
Alresford, Hants, SO24 9JH, UK
office1@jhpbooks.net
www.johnhuntpublishing.com
www.roundfire-books.com

For distributor details and how to order please visit the 'Ordering' section on our website.

Text copyright: Jeff Musillo 2013

ISBN: 978 1 78279 562 9

A CIP catalogue record for this book is available from the British Library.

Design: Lee Nash

Printed in the USA by Edwards Brothers Malloy

We operate a distinctive and ethical publishing philosophy in all
areas of our business, from our global network of authors to
production and worldwide distribution.

CONTENTS

Dedicated to my mother & Ashlyn

ALSO BY JEFF MUSILLO

The Ease of Access

Very Special Thanks to:
Steve Sturniolo, The Sisters of Charity, Eric Mausner, Aunt Dar,
Wendy Ott, and Aaron Taylor.

"The past is never dead. It's not even past."

– William Faulkner

VOLUME 1

EAST ORANGE, NEW JERSEY

Prologue

"Pour another fucking drink, you bastard," I heard someone howl from across the revolting room. Surrounded by mayhem and cracked walls covered in mysterious substances, I was in South Orange, New Jersey, in the midst of a disgraceful booze fest, feeling far from sober. I'd been going to these parties at least once a week for a few years by then. A friend of mine was a member of a fraternity at Seton Hall University. Everybody knew everybody, and they all treated me as a first-class ally.

I checked the clock on my cell phone. It was 2:40 a.m. I was standing on one side of a beer-pong table with my teammate, Steve. Our adversaries were standing at the other end. One of our rivals was Steve's stepbrother, Justin – a good friend and legal advisor of mine. His partner was. I really don't remember. We both had one cup left in our gin-pong match.

Justin and his partner had both missed their shots. It came to us. Steve missed his, but I made mine. Justin jokingly punted over the table of debauchery, which was holding the discarded red solo cups, a pitcher of beer, and an ashtray overflowing with cigarette butts. The table crashed loudly to the floor, drawing the attention of the drunks that were still in that garbage-filled house we called "Riggs."

A blunt was then passed around the room. I took a pull and suggested in my slurred speech that we go to the McDonald's in East Orange. It was open twenty-four hours a day.

"That's a fantastic idea," Steve mumbled.

I jumped into the car with Steve and Justin, and we were on our way. We drove down the bleak, poverty-stricken portion of South Orange Avenue. I had taken this trip many times, but on this night, my inquisitiveness was taking over. When we came upon East Orange, my questioning was becoming overwhelming. I wanted to know the truth about the bleak area. I wanted to know about the mindset of the people. I needed to know about the once-thriving city that turned into a remote ghetto.

I stayed silent in the back of the car and took everything in scenically: the gloomy streets and weakening walls festooned with graffiti tags showing people's names and people's crews. Derogatory statements painted on posters that displayed politicians' names. I observed expressively marooned people roaming the crumbling streets at what was now 3:00 a.m. on a Sunday morning. I was just an observer of these images...but not for long.

I had to go into the city. It was time for me to *be there*, which, when you think about it, is a scary thought. Being anywhere out of your zone of comfort is chilling. But at this point, it was absolutely vital. It is difficult to feel anything without passionately embracing that situation. It was time to learn.

Sadistic Sunshine
First Day
A Jehovah's Witness and a Pimp

The morning did not turn out as gracefully as I had hoped. I fell asleep around 4:30 a.m. and awoke about four hours later to thunderously loud members of my family. My grandparents were following my aunt and little cousin to their house in Virginia, and the opportune meeting place before starting that voyage was my house.

I am fond of the night. Mornings are not my thing. I think that I'm allergic to the sun. My vocal cords are so rarely in the best of shape anytime before noon. And if I could have screamed like a castrated lunatic when my grandmother booted in my bedroom door to shout her greetings and tell me, "Aunt Dar brought bagels!" believe me, I would have. I opened my mouth, but nothing came out.

After some more tossing and turning in my bed, I threw on some clothes and walked red-eyed past staring family members and to the refrigerator to get some orange juice. Someone had said something about not being a morning person, but I was too preoccupied with looking out the window for the morning paper. I couldn't see it in our driveway, so I asked my mother if it had come yet.

"Jeff, we haven't gotten the paper for five years."

"Good...it's full of lies," I told her. Then I buttered myself a bagel. It was the first time in a long time that I had breakfast. People say it's a jump-start to a good day. Normally, I could give two shits, but on that day, since it was my first day working on the book, I needed just that.

After a car ride of Tom Petty and chain-smoking cigarettes, I arrived around one o'clock in the afternoon in Orange, New

Jersey. I was driving on Main Street, trying to avoid a siren-blaring cop car with an ambulance tailing, both vehicles dodging civilians who were incautiously running across the street. Finally, I pulled into a parking spot, lit up another smoke, and sat back for a few minutes to observe.

Parked next to me was a still-running Honda Civic, exhaling smoke from its corroded tailpipe. A man was sitting in the driver's seat. The man was on the phone and had a look on his face that seemed to be one of dreadful rage. As I was getting my notebook and my wits together, I looked up to see a man walking on the sidewalk, approaching a Hispanic mother pushing her baby carriage. The man was an African-American who looked to be in his late twenties. He was a bit on the heavy side, unshaven, and wearing an oversized black North Face jacket.

Approaching the woman, he pulled his hand out from his jacket pocket and flashed a gold chain he was trying to sell. She shook her head from side to side signifying that she wasn't interested and continued on her way. The man did the same, while putting the chain back into his pocket.

All of a sudden, the man who was sitting in the Honda Civic next to me began to scream into his phone like a maniac. I could hear his muffled voice through both of our closed car windows. The dispute had something to do with money. He glanced over to me, and I just nodded. I got out of my car with my notebook and put a few hours' worth of change in the parking meter.

With no real place to start, I began to walk Main Street and peruse the stores. I stopped for a while when I came upon a stone testimonial with integrated children, a pleased-looking family, and a man playing saxophone painted on it.

Then, anticipating there would be East Orange citizens shopping on Main Street today, I started walking and gazing at what Orange had to offer. I was looking for the right time and the right person to start up my first conversation.

After about twenty minutes of strolling, I leaned up against a brick wall coated in graffiti, dividing a women's dress shop and an unreceptive-looking pub that had steel bars shielding the windows. I was watching the people that walked past me. The greater part of them did not give the most receptive glances towards me.

I stood at my tattered-brick-wall spot for about eight minutes just waiting for an opening. Fortunately, an elderly and petite African-American woman came up to me. Decked out in a long brown coat with glasses covering her entire face and a brown hat with a purple flower on the front of it, she was geared up for her day on the town. With an agreeable smile on her face, holding a stack of pamphlets, she came to me to see if I wanted one of her booklets. *Here's my first opening,* I thought to myself as she handed me two different pamphlets.

I told her why I was on Main Street and how I was trying to get a unique look into East Orange. I asked her if she was a resident of the city, which she was. She went on to tell me that she was in her eighties, and had been living in East Orange since she moved from Virginia in 1952. The small woman spoke in a particularly soft manner. I had to bend down to hear her better.

She told me she loved living in East Orange and that she had a couple of sons who lived in the city as well. I asked what she was doing on Main Street.

She pointed down to the pamphlets in my hand. One pamphlet was titled *The Watchtower: Announcing Jehovah's Kingdom.* The other was called *Awake.* It was about how the end of false religion was near. She cleared her throat and told me, "I'm out here today passing these out because Jesus is the only way. Jesus cared more about humanity than politics, so the people of Jesus should be that way as well."

She then said, "I don't trust politicians. They're all liars in my eyes. And I'm too old to be concerning myself with all that."

Then, unexpectedly, she opened up a little bit. "There's been a lot of tough times that folks had to endure around here. I'm not sure if politicians...if *anybody* cares too much about the people around here anymore. Like I said, I've been here for years now, and I can't go anywhere. I don't want to go anywhere, really. But these tough times are forming a whole new type of rough people. That's why I just follow the word of God instead of politics."

And that was that. The rendezvous was over. She said goodbye while shaking my hand and continued walking down the street trying to pass out pamphlets, "showing the way of God."

The Jehovah's Witness was very nice and showed me there were still people in the world getting their word out, whatever that word may be.

After the Jehovah's Witness walked off, I went over to a grimy trashcan on the sidewalk and used the rim as a writing table. I jotted down some notes while getting lost in the noise of Main Street. In the middle of writing some thoughts down, I looked up to see a guy staring at me. He quickly turned away. His age ranged from eighteen to twenty-four. He was African-American, and he was leaning his weight onto a cane he was holding.

I felt more confident after the conversation with the Jehovah's Witness, so I walked right up to him and introduced myself. His name was Antoine. He seemed a bit diffident. The first few minutes of our discussion, he would only briefly look me at me then look away. He was standing in front of a store that sold cell phones, and he kept glimpsing inside the store to monitor the customers.

Following our awkward introduction, he started speaking about how he was an aspiring rapper from East Orange, but the city didn't have the recording capabilities that Newark did, so he frequently took trips there to record. He compared East Orange to Newark a lot. His tone was spiteful when he went on to say, "There are just more opportunities in Newark...which means less money in East Orange." Suddenly, our discussion came to a halt when he saw there weren't any more customers in the store.

He held up a cell phone in his free hand and told me, "I've gotta go sell this shit. Don't leave. I'll be right back."

Antoine came back out after a minute or so, disappointedly shaking his head, suggesting his trip was a failure. He told me to follow him because he knew a man who would want the phone. We walked up the block, which appeared to be a challenge for him due to his limping. I asked him what happened to his leg and he told me, "I fucked it up jumping out the window, running from the cops."

We stopped again about ten feet from where we were originally standing, and Antoine went on talking about the police in East Orange. He told me that there was a lot of hassle from the cops. He stated, "I understand that their job is to bust up illegal shit, but they gotta understand that not everybody is a fucking criminal...I don't know, man. There's a lot of people in this city that look alike, so maybe they just get confused." He sounded defeated. Then he told me again he'd be right back and hobbled into the other cell phone store.

This time, with a grin on his face, Antoine emerged from the store. He shuffled over to me and whispered that he sold the cell phone for five dollars. "I could've sold that shit for twenty-five, but fuck it, five is better than nothing." He snickered before blasting into a speech about East Orange. "It's just a way of life out here, man, you know? Everybody *has* to make money. That's a fact. I *gotta* find what people will buy. I just sold that cell phone, boom, that's five bucks! Now, I won't be hungry today. I cut my man's lawn last week, so he owes me twenty."

He wavered for a few seconds, shook another man's hand that walked past, and turned back to me to continue, "Everybody has to be part of something, right? I mean, look at me." That's when he rolled up the sleeve of his red shirt to show the tattoo on his right forearm affiliating him with the street gang, The Bloods. "You see that? But that don't mean we can't be civil. If we could be civil, then we could stop the fucking violence. I mean, I got this tattoo on my arm, *right*? But I still go to the park and do my little pushups and shit with Crips, and they ain't said shit. I wear my red beads and workout with them, because I know them, and they know me. East Orange ain't that big of a place. A lot of people be bumping into each other, and sometimes, that ain't good...

"... But we understand each other, and we don't *have* to be violent...and that could be a good thing for the city. They know I can be all-good, and we can workout together, or whatever, and there don't have to be a problem. But I'm a pimp, so we don't have to worry about shit anyways." He then laughed and said, "I'm gonna limp my ass back to the crib, smoke a blunt, and stare at the clouds."

Business is Business
Disturbing Peace

Back on Main Street in Orange, New Jersey. The street filled with self-made, non-corporate businesses covering the sidewalks. One after another, they were all right next to each other, cramped and dull. In the span of a five-minute walk, you could shop for tunes at the Orange Music Emporium, get a wig or hair dye at Mimi's Hair and Wigs, stop off for some food at Lisa's Deli, and then get some knickknacks at 99 Cent Dreams.

While watching Main Street's workforce, I see the tremendous struggle seep out of the people. There is an intense do-or-die mentality here... There has to be.

Everyone is out to get that buck. Businessmen and business-women, no matter where they fall on the spectrum of commerce, are full of zeal. Their hearts bleed green, and their blood rushes every time they hear the sound of the *ding-dong* bell. But sometimes there is great nervousness. I came face to face with an uneasy employee when I walked into a tiny eatery called Trinidad Style Restaurant.

Prior to going into the eatery, I stood outside while a woman dressed in a tattered purple coat was scoping the shelves for food. I decided to wait outside the restaurant until the woman bought her chow. The woman purchased something with a hand full of coins and went to eat in the small sit-down area in the restaurant. The time was right. I went in for some "Q&A"...or at least the "Q" part.

When I walked in, an older Korean woman stood up from a stool behind the counter and asked me if I "needed something."

I explained to her what I was doing and asked if I could get some information about the restaurant. She started flailing her hands and her English became broken as she choked out, "I don't know...no, not me...uhh. Wait, I...uh...get someone." She walked to the back of the store and brought out an irate-looking Pakistani man, about six feet tall and sporting a fuzzy five o'clock shadow and a stained apron. He came towards me and asked what the trouble was.

"No trouble at all. I'm writing a book about East Orange..." He cut me off. "This is not East Orange. East Orange is down that way," he said sternly as he pointed.

"I know that," I told him, "but today I'm writing about the businesses on Main Street that citizens from East Orange might come to. So maybe you could give me some information about your restaurant here." I said this rather hastily, which seemed to terrify him. He threw his hands in the air. He banged his hands on the counter in annoyance and perplexity. The scene was getting tense.

"I don't know, man, the boss ain't here. I'm not the boss. I mean, yeah, of course people from East Orange come here to eat. But why do you want to know anything about this place, anyway?" he asked with his hands planted on his hips and terror in his eyes.

"No worries, man...Uhhh, how long has this place been open? Do you know that?"

"Seven years. Go talk to the boss. He works at the other store down the street, the one by Walgreens."

I agreed and thanked him for his time. I watched him from the corner of my eye staring at me and nervously looking back to his Korean coworker while I walked out of the store.

And, instead of going toward Walgreens, I walked down the street and situated myself outside of a liquor store called Double Dee. I stood there for a while smoking and watching people run up and down the street. Some seemed to have imperative agendas. Some were noticeably drugged up, leisurely and aimlessly on the move for mysterious intentions.

On the corner of the street, a few feet from Double Dee, there was construction going on. Big mounds of dirt and a heavy-duty bulldozer were taking up the whole corner. Some of the staff were working. Some were joking around. One employee put up a makeshift "Do Not Enter" sign on the corner, which proved to be meaningless because I witnessed eight people walk up to the sign, stare uninterestedly, and jump over it to stomp through the disorder.

It was now 1:30 in the afternoon. Double Dee Liquors was getting a profusion of people coming and going to and from the store. Some with cases of beer. Others with plastic bags filled with assorted clanking bottles.

On my way in, I bumped into an elderly man sporting a long gray beard. He came rushing out of the store walking hurriedly. His face glowing with hopeful optimism. A scratch-off lottery ticket in his hand. Sometimes all it takes is the hope to keep us alive.

Double Dee was around fifteen feet long with enough width for a person to turn around uncomfortably. The store didn't have a lot of merchandise. The shelves were virtually bare.

The second thing I noticed, after the measurements of the store, was a Middle Eastern man, wearing a white and gold colored silk buttoned-down shirt, with a gold chain around his neck and the pendant buried under his mattress of chest hair. He was working the register. Next to him was a younger Hispanic woman sitting on an aged wooden chair, reading a book.

She only looked up in my direction once, then back to the book, and remained in that position for the duration of my time at Double Dee. Lounging on the counter next to the cash register was a wiry Hispanic male in his teens, dressed in all blue, covered in tattoos, scratching off a lottery game.

At first, the three in the liquor store paid me no attention, probably thinking that I was just looking around for booze. I waited for the Middle Eastern man to look up and then started with the introductions. I told him that I'd like to ask him and the other employees about working here. He told me that he was the only member of the staff. "Oh, I'm sorry, you don't work here?" I asked the Hispanic male. He quickly hopped off the counter, shook his head no, and walked with his scratch-off to the other end of the store.

Everyone in the store was just as guarded as the stained-apron man at the Trinidad Style Restaurant. There was a discomforting feeling that made the walls of the already narrow space feel as if they were closing in on me. There was also a hostile sentiment that if I wasn't buying anything, I should get the hell out of there.

But before I split I did get some information out of the Double Dee cashier. After a little prying, he told me that he enjoyed working there because it wasn't uptight. "That's why I've been here for seven years. There's no real hassles." When I asked if he lived in East Orange, he sneered and spoke in a palpable tone, "I can't live in no East Orange, man, too dangerous." He said that he commuted in every day.

"From where?"

He would not tell me that. Nor did he tell me his name. But he did tell me that, "Prime time is Friday. That's when we make out money-wise. Friday afternoon, we'll get some good action, and sometimes, when the night comes around, we see the same people that were here a few hours before. People like to get liquored. I mean, look at the guy right there." He pointed outside to a man in worn-out clothing sitting on the sidewalk curb brown-bagging it.

While I was looking at the man outside, my vision suddenly became blocked by two men who entered wearing matching outfits with "Engineer" stitched over the left breast. They pulled out two Budweiser tall boys from Double Dee's refrigerator, walked in front of me as if I was invisible, put them on the counter, and started having a conversation with the cashier. They seemed to know each other. Maybe the engineers were everyday patrons.

I figured that it was time to leave. As miniscule as the conversation was, I was still content with the overall feeling...even though it was one of distrust. I waved goodbye and he just nodded. Business was more important than any conversation with me. I understood that perfectly.

Just from a couple of unreceptive conversations on Main Street, I found the prevalent consensus with the businesses seemed to be that *time is money and you're wasting my time.* The members of staff did not give the impression of caring where anyone was from or what their life story was. It was a buy-something-or-be-gone state of mind. They had a job to do. And that job had nothing to do with a city that may or may not be "too dangerous" unless the citizens of that city were clientele.

On my way back to my car, I stopped by the Orange Public Library. The library was, of course, quiet and passive. Nevertheless, it was beyond doubt an astounding place. Sometimes, you don't realize the magnificence of certain things until you have been in an area that is strictly filled with activity. I was really excited to have the hushed surroundings of a library. The opportunity to hear my own thoughts. Noises will always be more piercing and more constant in a city that is in an unvarying state of urgency.

Initially, the library seemed small and cozy. About five feet from the front door, I saw a round desk where two older African-American librarians were working. To the left was a room with a handful of desks. To the right, I saw another wing with three rows of computers and one more desk, behind which a Hispanic librarian with her hair in an untidy bun was sitting.

I continued to walk around the round desk in the middle and came to see that the library was actually quite large. Looking around, I saw rows upon rows of seasoned shelves that were too small, containing the overflowing books. I carried on. Saw the sights. And then noticed there was a second floor. The library became extravagant to me. I went back to where the librarian was still engrossed in activity, and, just to start up a conversation, I asked her if she could help me find *The Collective Works of Allen Ginsberg*. I actually had the book in the backseat of my car, which made me think of it.

She looked up with her pale eyes and told me that she would help me find it. We walked around and searched for my request. She was an obliging woman who went on to tell me that the library was always full in the morning with senior citizens. "They come on in here and read the paper and socialize. It's really nice." She also informed me that about three o'clock, Monday through Friday, the library became crowded with youthful study groups from both Orange and East Orange. "This place gives kids something else to look forward to. Many college kids come here to get jobs as well. It's a positive place." She said this as we came up negative on the Ginsberg search. I told her that the library was gorgeous and thanked her for her help.

Prior to leaving, I told her I was working on this book and she seemed fascinated. "We need something like that," she replied speaking about East Orange. "We need more people to know what's going on in these areas. There are good people here, but a lot of negative things still take place here. And it's those harmful situations that make people afraid to lend a helping hand. People can only do so much with so little." She then wished me good luck and we parted ways. I got into my car and drove to my friend's house in West Orange.

I arrived at the house in West Orange, a place we call "The Rock", which was empty, at around 5:00 p.m. I had a couple of hours to kill before I had to be in New York. I was going to the city to meet with a group of people to hit a few bars.

Once I got myself settled in the vacant house, I tried to read some of my Ginsberg book. But I couldn't focus, beset as I was with confused contemplations. The whole house was empty. If there was a time to unwind, it was then. Instead, I walked around chain-smoking, drinking beer, randomly staring out the window. I started thinking about the people I had come across today. I wondered if they were enjoying a peaceful moment or if their minds were too hectic to unwind.

Holy Shit, Man...Cops Everywhere!
Wanna Get High?
Overcast of Violence

As I arrived in East Orange, waiting to see what kind of cards I was dealt for the day, the first thing I witnessed was a pleasant-looking young couple walking down the street with their hands intertwined. They were enjoying the brisk and breezy December morning. Who knows where they were going. But who cares. They seemed to be content.

Zoom! I snapped out of my trance when one, two, three cop cars went speeding past me, sirens blaring and echoing in my ears like loud techno music. There was always a serious presence of police in East Orange, but since I started this book, I had never seen this much activity. Wondering what was going on, I began walking down Martin Luther King Boulevard, on the road to the same place the cops were heading.

I got about twenty feet down the block before I heard someone scream from across the street, "Yo, man! Hold up!" I looked up to see an African-American man, sporting ragged clothes, unkempt facial hair, and a missing front tooth running towards me with his untied shoelaces flopping on the punctured concrete. "Hey, man, what's up?" he asked me as we shook hands. Before I could answer, his tall lean frame let out a peculiar spasm, and his next question came torpedoing out of his mouth in halting sentences. "Hey, man! Wanna get high? You smoke? Wait! You a cop?"

"Nah, I'm not a cop."

"Cool, man! Let's get high."

I said I was good at that moment and told him I was writing a story on East Orange.

"Oh, shit!" he replied. Before he could start telling me things, a man came out from a dreary, unwelcoming building that was ten feet away from us. He came out of the door and started screaming at the man I was talking with. No stores surrounded the construction he surfaced from, which seemed to be an apartment building with no labeling numbers on the door.

The seething man that came out of this stranded building was wearing a bloody chef's apron. He again screamed for the man I was talking with. The Wanna-get-high man jerked quickly and turned around to tell the irate man to wait a minute. He then turned back to me and just started rattling off numbers. "7432, 874, 25, 8962..." While he was bellowing out these digits, he got awkwardly close to me and started popping the collar on my army fatigue jacket.

He continued to shout numbers. I couldn't make out if they were in some sort of systematic order, or if he was just rambling. While this carried on, I put down my collar to see if he would notice... He did. He insisted on popping it again. He kept on rattling and popping my collar. At last, I realized that he was just listing off the addresses of all the houses that he had lived in before. I somehow also made out through his vigorous and enthusiastic speech that at this moment, he was living on both North and South Clinton Street. "I gotta stay on the move, man." Then he screamed, "They can't catch *me*, baby!"

"What the fuck!" the man in the bloody apron screamed from down the block.

"Oh, shit, alright, man, I gotta get going. Remember that shit, though. I lived in Newark till I was four but came to this mother-fucker because it's wild, and I love it!" He was yelling all of this while keeping eye contact with me and walking backwards towards the man and the daunting building. It wasn't really walking, though. It was some sort of pulsating sway/backwards electric slide up the sidewalk.

Strolling down Martin Luther King Boulevard, which seemed to have churches on almost every corner, I noticed that besides the heavy presence of police, there wasn't much action going on today. As I considered this, a loud roar of a fire-truck siren went off behind me. I turned around to see two fire trucks whizzing past me. I wondered what was going on. It must have been something pretty intense.

I walked for a while, passing only a couple of people who did not look like they were in the mood for any sort of interaction. Plus, I couldn't find where those cop cars had raced off to. I turned back around and started walking in the direction of my starting point. Unexpectedly, I heard, for a second time from across the street, "Yo, man!" I looked up and saw my collar-popping friend running like an excited child towards me. "Come on! Let's get high," he said, and we started walking towards the Brick Church train station. He was rattling off some more numbers, this time with no breath in between. "632970528739 15570529…you know what I'm saying?"

I told him, "Not really," and without faltering, he skipped to the next topic that was on his mind.

"I gotta jump these trains, man. I jumped three last week! I didn't have no money to ride, but I gotta get to where I gotta go, you know?" I asked him where he had to go. "Fuck that! It doesn't really matter. I just have people to see, you dig? I'm alright and all that, but not much money in these pockets. You need a bag!?" I shook my head no. "Fuck it, baby! I do what I gotta do to survive, ya dig? It's that life! I didn't create it, but I'm here, ain't I?"

It was a fast walk to the train station. We stopped in front of the stairs that led up to the tracks. He took one more long pull off his Kool cigarette, stomped it out with his unlaced boot, and asked me for one of my cigarettes and five dollars. I gave him a smoke and buck and told him to make sure he got where he was going. "Oh, I always get where I'm going, baby! I'm going to see my girl. I love the little lady, and she love me! Like I said, no money or not, I'ma gets to where I gotta go! Maybe I'll marry her," he said this as if he was asking himself. "Eh, who gives a fuck, right? I don't need no ring. I might be crazy! But we keep each other in control. It's a damn disgrace I gotta jump these trains to see her, but you gotta do what you gotta do!" We slapped hands goodbye, and he hurriedly jumped/levitated up the steps to his train. We never got high together, but you never know what the future holds.

Afterthought:

I found out later there was a shooting in East Orange at the same time I was in the neighborhood, which clarifies the serious police activity. I stopped by my friend's house at around midnight, and he told that it was on the news all day. Normally, I would've wanted to know what happened. Who got shot, and what was it over? But I just didn't have the stomach to find out. Sure, I was physically close to the area where the shooting took place, but emotionally, I felt even closer.

Last Day
Stroll Down Hazy Lane
Recollections that Led to Revelation

It was a cold morning in January. I awoke, feeling nothing but misery, on the floor of my friend's West Orange house—The Rock—plagued by obscure memories of last night's excessive drinking. I hazily remembered only flashing moments of the night before. I remembered when we took the first shot of whiskey. I remembered walking crookedly into a South Orange bar, smuggling beers in my oversized army fatigue jacket. And I remembered jumping over a chain link fence on the way home. Why did I jump over the fence? I don't remember that. My friend's cell phone alarm was blaring the song "Renegade" by Styx.

The jig is up, the news is out, they've finally found me
The renegade who had it made, retrieved for a bounty.

"Not me, my friend, but all right, I'm awake." I stood up from where I was lying and realized I had a throbbing hangover. *Fuck it, nothing a soda and some cold air can't cure,* I thought to myself while retrieving my eyeglasses concealed inside of my filthy Timberland boots. I stretched, cracked my neck, and left for East Orange.

I was fortunate today. Right from the get-go I ran into a man who was standing by himself in front of a store called Hood Clothing. He was a sharp-looking African-American man with partially gray hair cropped close to his head. He was wearing blue jeans with a black flight jacket covering a black shirt. And I was soon to find out he was quite the poignant rollercoaster of a person. I wasted no time immediately introducing myself to him and learning that his name was Morgan.

Morgan was a hasty yet polite man at the age of thirty-two. "I lived here my whole life," he said in a rapid verbal punch. I could see that he was an intelligent man who did not have the appetite for bullshit.

"What're you doing out here?" he had asked me in a paranoid manner.

I told him about the book. Mentioned I was interested in any sort of information or feelings he could provide.

"A book about East Orange! What for? Can't you see everybody forgot about us, man?" He said this while looking at the surroundings. He asked me what I was writing about. I figured I'd just go for the neck.

I told him it was a book on politics and the community of East Orange.

"Politics!" He laughed. "Get the fuck outta here. What politics? Wait, better question, what *politicians*?" He stared at me intensely, waited for a response, and then continued, "Honestly, you think politicians are dying to give us a helping hand here? I'm not saying I need help...from anyone, but I mean come on, look around! Those fucks ain't worried about the ghetto, at least not this one. I mean, look at that Katrina shit, you see how long it took them to get going on that shit, and that was a *public* issue! Fuck!"

He let out a scoff and then proceeded by speaking on gentrification. "There's cities being revamped all over this country, but you know, there is money to be made with that shit. But the *people* don't see any of that shit. When they rebuild the ghetto and make some nice houses, they up the prices, and the people that was there before can't afford to go back...fuck that," he said solemnly.

"But I chill here. I love it here. This is my place. I don't wanna be one of those guys that bitches about the ghetto, but..." He paused again and then asked me if I listened to rap. I told him I did, and he said, "Alright, take that for example. I like how there are black people taking negative things, spinning that shit, and making shit more positive, you know, a street poetry type deal. But sometimes, that shit can be no good. You know, to be constantly talking about killing and robbing, in the long run, only makes shit worse. I mean don't get me wrong, I think it's necessary for some of these other people to really know what the hell is going on in the ghetto. But I also think it's time to grow."

We walked over to the front steps of a house where a group of four, tough-looking African-American teenagers were standing around, bullshitting with each other. The group took a long look at me, glanced over to Morgan, and nodded back towards my direction. "Nah, he's good," Morgan told the group, motioning for me to sit with him on the front steps of the house. The group moved down the block away from us. I lit up a stick.

It became a gorgeous afternoon, although still a bit cold from the morning winds. There was less of a breeze on this block, which made it enjoyable to just sit around and let Morgan express himself. He took a blunt out of the pocket of his black flight jacket, inspected it, then spoke like a cruel wise man. "Ya know, those kids would've ripped the heart outta ya chest, right?" I looked back at him taking a few seconds to think of the proper way to answer that question.

"But you look like a kid that could defend himself." All I told him was that I would have.

Morgan leisurely nodded while looking down at his tarnished black boots. He spit on the cracked concrete, let out a low sigh, and lit the blunt. He took a couple of pulls, passed it to me, and began to speak his mind. "It's not a black and white thing. Not anymore, not with me anyways. I can't really speak on those guys," he said pointing to the group who were now at the other corner of the block, still gazing back at Morgan and me. "But it *is* a territory thing, ya know? People get sketched when they see a new face come around, especially a type of face they not used to seeing."

I passed him back the blunt and asked him why he thought

23

people's mentality, in general, was like that. He took a lengthy drag, smoke covered his face, and he went on in a manner a lot calmer than the one from before. "In general? I don't know about general, man. I know about the ghetto. I know bout this shit right here." Morgan's aggression started to return. "I know that we don't have much around here, and when we feel like there's somebody trespassing, we gotta protect our shit. It's as simple as that...

"... But we gotta lot of heart out here. People...and the news and shit might portray us, and other areas like us, in a bad ways or whatever. But we know who we are, we know what we got. And we know what we need. But if you want clarity for whatever story you're writing, I'm sorry to tell you, you ain't gonna get it. You can't get clarity from people who have real questions but receive no answers themselves. You know what I'm sayin'? I don't know, man, maybe we be territorial because a lot of us feel as if we were robbed... We still getting robbed.

"The thing that hurts the ghetto is that we not only getting robbed out of opportunities, but we gettin' robbed emotionally, too. So we do what we gotta do to get ours and survive."

We both stared straight ahead and finished smoking in silence.

Feeling a bit lofty, I was driving around before going home. By chance, I ended up back on Main Street. I parked and went into the Orange Public Library to see if I could find the librarian who tried to locate the Ginsberg book. She was there helping somebody out. She glanced up at me and smiled. She then led the woman she was assisting in the appropriate direction and came up to me asking if I had found "that, uh, *Ginsberg book*?"

I was surprised she remembered and told her that I did find it. She asked if she could help me out with anything else. I told her I was fine, and I was just getting out of the cold. She smiled and told me the finest thing I had heard in a while. "Okay then, well good luck on that book you're writing." I was taken aback, but I managed to peep out a thank you.

I remember leaving the library feeling rejuvenated, feeling like I just wanted to finish this volume and get it out to anybody that would read it. I felt blessed, due to the city of East Orange, with a large invigorating and influential shock that brought me back to life. The things I have seen, the people I have met, and the words I have heard I will never forget.

VOLUME 2

NEW ORLEANS, LOUISIANA

Prologue

Frequently referred to as "the most unique city," New Orleans has exhibited that matchlessness ever since its American birth. No one can deny that "The Crescent City" strived to be different from the time of its derivation, especially when it came to labor. Given that the city is a chief port for North America, New Orleans had a leading role in the Slave Trade during the 19th Century. Conversely, due to its individuality and progressiveness, New Orleans was a Confederate city striving for egalitarianism, and included flourishing opportunities for every ethnicity, which was highly contentious for the southern states at that juncture. By the time the city of distinctiveness had become part of the Union, it had developed into the wealthiest and third-most populous city in the nation, continually striving toward unique fulfillment.

This land of Louisiana is also known as the *Big Easy*. In fact, a number of people have said that the appellation perhaps derived from the easiness to find work in New Orleans. There are also accounts that the name may have originated at some point during the Prohibition era, since New Orleans was considered one huge speak-easy, supplying exuberance and making it simple to clash against the rules of the 18th Amendment. Whatever the case may be, thanks to what I experienced throughout my own time there, I began calling New Orleans the Big Easy simply because of the upbeat acceptance exhibited by its citizens.

On a depressing note, New Orleans regularly had to be conscious of the peril of detrimental hurricanes. And as everyone knows, at the end of August 2005, Hurricane Katrina came storming in, causing not only the nastiest civil-engineering catastrophe in American history, but also atrocious tragedy and the loss of many lives. Yet, although there was heartbreak, I would soon ascertain that the hurricane did not inject lost hope.

"I gotta get down there," I told my mother at five a.m. on a July morning.

"Where now?" she replied.

"New Orleans. I want to talk to the people down there."

"Jeff, it's been two years...so, hopefully...they're back on track."

"*Hopefully*. That's the key word. There's only one way to find out for sure."

My mother let out a long sigh then, being the encouraging person she has always been, she said, "Well, I guess I could talk to the sister for you."

"Aunt Dar knows somebody down there?"

"Not *my* sister. Sister Pat from Saint Catherine's church."

My mother didn't hesitate. Within a couple of days, I was filling out paperwork, getting a tetanus shot, and becoming linked up with a religious group of nuns and volunteers called the *Sisters of Charity*, a group that would be flying me down to the Big Easy and putting a roof over my head. What the hell, right? Me, some nuns, New Orleans, it all seemed like a journey I'd never forget.

I was ready. Ready and equipped to hop on a plane, position myself between two keen wings, and ascend toward fresh visuals. I was eager, beyond amped up to discover why New Orleans is also called "The City That Care Forgot."

Extra Baggage
Introducing Mr. McNasta
The Arrival, The Commencement

Planes were soaring as I attempted to remain focused and wait for my flight. But this is a tricky objective when one is walking around Newark airport. Very challenging when one hears a malicious beast threaten a 17-year-old McDonald's employee about food not currently being served.

"Give me some fucking hot cakes, son, or I'll eat your damn retinas instead!"

Along with that insanity, there was a confounded couple over my right shoulder, a duo attempting to teach each other the ways of the Spanish language.

I zoned in and heard the man say, "Que? I told you before...I *need* the window seat. I must see everything! I'm always the navigator."

The woman responded, "Pardon? We'll be on a damn airplane. How in the hell are you going to navigate? You gonna jump in the cockpit, Captain Dickhead?

"Ahhhh, Chupaverga!"

"Eh, vete a carajo!"

It was time for my flight.

I sometimes receive many questions. Because of that, I tend to repeat myself a lot. Ironically enough, repetition is something I loathe. It is so exasperating for me to repeat myself that I, on certain days, just make shit up. I have to just to keep myself stimulated. The flight to New Orleans was one of those times.

I was the only person from our group not sitting next to one of the New Orleans aids, which meant I sat in the window seat next to a couple of young, smartly dressed Indian gentlemen. It wasn't until takeoff that I discovered they were not only a couple of curious questioners, but also a couple of assholes. I was reading an article story about an execution-style killing that had just taken place in Newark, N.J. when the Indian man sitting in the aisle seat spoke in a haughty tone, "Excuuuuse me!"

I didn't look up at first.

"I said, Exc*uuuuuuuuu*se me."

I looked away from the article and toward a strange sight. My two co-passengers were just staring at me. The man in the middle remained silent, a smug look on his face, as the man in the aisle seat brought on the investigation.

"Tattoos?" he complacently asked.

"Huh?"

"Are those *real* tattoos?" he questioned.

"Real tattoos?" I asked pointing down to my arms. "Ya. These are real tattoos."

"How long?" he pompously questioned.

"What are you talking about? The length?"

"No." He scoffed while grabbing the other man's forearm and snickering. "How long do they last?"

"Oh. Forever."

"What kind of allergies come with having those...*things*? Are they poisonous?"

He nuzzled his face into the other man's neck and began laughing. I felt it was the right moment to go off on a bizarre course. Also, since my tattoos are emblematic and significant to me, I wanted to evade the opening of my true feelings to these assholes.

"Poisonous? Not mine, my friend. But some people get rare cases of what is called, 'The ghastly poison tattoo'." I told him.

"Really, the...poison tat...too?"

"Damn right. Poison," I shot back. "Have you ever seen a man shit blood?"

"Like, uh, from his asshole?"

"No from his eyeballs. Yes, of course from his **ASSHOLE!**" I dramatically whispered. "One time, I saw a man get a tattoo needle put into his vein. Shit, that wicked ink lived on. Forever in his bloodstream."

Both of the men sitting next to me looked horrified. They wanted out. But it was too late for that. I guess they should have sprung for first class.

I proceeded, "The man who got the needle in his vein, after discovering why he kept leaving his toilet bowl all bloody, came back to the tattoo parlor where he'd been infected, right, and took a bloody diarrhea shit all over the walls. It was a chilling scene. The bloody shit sprayed everywhere and ended up covering an innocent 17-year-old girl, some little teenager who was there with her mother. The poor girl was their getting her belly button pierced for a birthday present. The police arrested the 'Bloody Asshole' and had him committed to an insane asylum."

I jabbed the forearm of the man closest to me to see if he still had a functioning brain.

"I can't believe that," the man sitting in the aisle seat finally spurted out, losing his patronizing attitude.

"Well believe it, guy. There are still bloody shit stains covering the parlor's walls. Not to mention, similar cases of the 'Bloody Asshole' are all around the world."

"Oh my God, that's awful. Good thing *we* don't have tattoos. Geez…after story like that, I think, I think I should know your name," he messily said.

"I'm Ignacious McNasta," I told him while extending my arm for a handshake. "My friends call me Shasta."

A bit baffled he asked, "*Shasta*? What is it you do, Shasta?"

"I tell dirty stories."

When the plane landed at the Louis Armstrong New Orleans International Airport, the two men hurried off as fast as they possibly could, and I, along with the other New Jersey aids met the additional members of our volunteer group.

I was in a new state; pleased that I avoided the act of opening my soul to two strangers. Ready to lend a hand and get to work. But little did I know how much I would be face to face with personal exposure during my time in New Orleans. I would soon learn about the challenges of understanding my own mentality. I had no clue I was about to be involved in an overwrought mêlée with myself. A battle that would rupture my fortified walls and force me to rebuild my confidence.

Rinse Out with Morning Surprise
Look Out Below

I was awake by 7:40 a.m. My first morning in New Orleans. Given that I was sharing a room with three other strangers—later to be four—I was finally ready to begin my day by about 8:10. I was uneasy since I was splitting a tight spot with unfamiliar people. I am big on having personal space. It helps me get my thoughts together. But I knew that was not going to occur at all during my week in the Big Easy.

But I was willing to work with what I had.

Our faction of volunteers set up shop at an apartment complex called Mater Dolorosa School, located on Carrollton Street. For the most part, the building housed senior citizens who seemed to be in high spirits, especially when seeing fresh faces.

I was the last person from my room to join the volunteer group in the kitchen. I was en route to the refrigerator to get the peanut butter sandwich I had packed the night before when I heard that someone would be treating the whole group to a meal later that day.

"Nice, I guess we'll just get going then," I said, tossing my sad-looking sandwich back inside the refrigerator.

"Not until we pray," one of my co-volunteers said with a smile.

Everybody rose from their chairs and looked at the ground. It was a sight that left me surprised. I never claimed to be a religious man, especially when it came to being aggressive with only one religion. But I have always thought of myself as someone with a strong spiritual sentiment. In some cases, being religious and being spiritual are two entirely different things. This was one of those cases.

With everybody's hands intertwined, one of the nuns started her prayers for those who had undergone anguish due to

Hurricane Katrina. She prayed for the people who had passed on. The people forced to flee. The people that we would all be assisting on our first morning in New Orleans. While listening to the prayer, I took a moment to glace around the humming kitchen. I looked at the sisters and all of the tender volunteers. Everybody had their heads humbly hanging. Everybody was in physical harmony and gentleness, yet, everybody was in mental distress.

Following the prayer service, all of the volunteers divvied up and crammed into the various vehicles driven by the nuns. They weren't dressed in their nun garments—but you can picture that if it helps. Our initial stop on the over-100-degree summer day was a deserted retirement center called the Nazareth Inn. The Nazareth Inn was comprised of two structures basically in the middle of nowhere.

After a quick introduction with one of the building's maintenance men, an elderly African-American who spoke in an easygoing manner, we split up once more into different groups, this time consisting of generally five people to each division. The maintenance man assigned each group to a floor in one of the buildings. Our designated floors were where we'd be carrying out our tasks.

Our obligations were to go into the rooms on our floors and get rid of the old, corroding furniture. Possessions abandoned by escaping residents as Katrina marked her brutal path. Keep in mind, this trip to New Orleans was in August of 2007, meaning these apartments had hardly been touched for nearly two years. So they were filthy.

Out of the Nazareth Inn's five floors, my group worked on the third. Uncomfortably dressed in a baggy, long sleeve T-shirt, dirty blue jeans, work boots, and borrowed brown wool gloves, I made my way to the first room in need of sanitizing. When I marched through that entryway, I saw chaotic disorder.

The room's smudged walls bordered the clutter of broken

cabinets, cracked dressers, ripped cushions, flipped chairs, stained carpets, and, oddly enough, absolute hollowness. If you spent a week in this room, before the hurricane hit, and had the job of obliterating everything, you wouldn't come close to the quantity of damage the storm had inflicted. I was standing in tainted devastation. I was standing in years of disregarded grime. I was standing in someone's home.

Ideally, by cleaning out these ruined apartments, the volunteers were giving the chance for somebody else to come in and make it their new home. So with the idea of new beginnings in mind, I put on those cheap wool gloves and prepared myself to get to work.

But before we started removing the dilapidated furniture our now smaller work-group of four girls, myself and a nun, got together, joined hands, and prayed for the former occupant. Tears filled the nun's eyes as she spoke. I could see that she truly felt pain in her heart. It was a remarkable sight. It's not every day that I get to encounter such warmth from someone feeling pain over a complete stranger's sorrow.

Following the prayer, the group worked collectively to remove all garbage and pick up the hefty furnishings to move it down a stretched hallway and onto a cramped balcony. Every floor had a balcony. So as soon as I paced outside I heard the sound of boisterous bedlam. The majority of the volunteers were outside on their balconies, screaming and making their own plans with their furniture.

My group was in the middle. Two balconies over our section, two underneath. As a form of warning, members from the other groups screamed the number of the floor they were on and dropped the bulky furniture off their balcony and into a dumpster located on the grass below.

It was the only way to get the furniture out of the building. I have no clue how the former residents got their furnishings inside. At one point, I was trying to maneuver a massive wooden drawer and line it up perfectly so I could have it plunge unwaveringly into the dumpster. Feeling the woodchips of the decaying drawer prick my palms, I screamed as soon as I felt confident I would not miss...

"FLOOR THREE!!!"

The drawer left our balcony and descended with great momentum toward the dumpster. Within seconds, it sailed over the planned target and smashed on the untrimmed grass a few feet away from the intended target. My misses, which happened frequently, would later lead to me cleaning the shattered pieces on the ground.

That is how our morning went. It was amusing to toss the furniture from such great heights. But when we became too carried away we stopped and thought how that furniture used to belong to someone who was forced to escape. That consciousness usually hit us when we finished cleaning one room and moved on to another.

After a few hours and a few rooms, the whole group gathered outside and discussed the morning's events. I sat in the shade and enjoyed a couple of cigarettes. I thought about the folks that used to live in that apartment complex. Wondered where they all went.

Following the stoppage of chitchat, we went back to our vehicles and drove off to a different retirement center: Metairie Manor. This is where we'd have a nice break for some much-needed lunch. Everyone in the car was drained and hushed. We all gave our sweat to the soil. The soil was noticeably munificent as well. It made its mark on all of our bodies.

We arrived at Metairie Manor at around 12:30 p.m. The blazing New Orleans sun was still hitting us hard. Everyone's pace was sluggish. After an incredibly slow walk through the parking lot, we were all thrilled to get into an air-conditioned building and have some food. In the vast dining area of the retirement center were some residents lining up to get themselves lunch as well. It must have been one helluva vision for the residents to witness the group of volunteers enter the room: a collection of grimy young adults meandering through their building, covered in sweat, dirt and random debris.

All the residents had smiles on their faces. It seemed like they had known us for years. As if we were their own grandchildren. While walking to the table for lunch I had heard one of the residents say, "It's so nice to know the young ones still come by to help. It's so nice to see that people still care."

I felt revitalized after our lunch. Recharged to the point where I could get up and go outside for a smoke.

I lit up and read a story in the local paper about the wreckage caused by Katrina. I read about the debris still in the lakes of New Orleans, demolishing the local fishers' income and general way of life. One man had said to a reporter, "I've wrecked two of my boats riding up on some big debris. So now, I got to go out of my way to get around the shards. And the areas I go to now is hardly ever good for crabbing. My business has definitely suffered."

While finishing the article, a few members from the volunteer group walked outside and put on their gloves. I figured we were going back to Nazareth Inn so I gave a curious nod.

"We're gonna rip out some of these weeds in front of the building here," one volunteer said in his Ohio tone.

"Right on," I responded while getting off the concrete and putting on my soggy gloves. In no time, all the volunteers were outside putting in work on Metairie Manor's front garden. By the end of the second hour, our bodies were sodden with encumbering mud. My filthy hair stuck to my face.

Even though the procedure was small, I truly felt we were lending a supportive hand. Every time a resident came outside they were glowing with exuberance, each person happier than the last. Every tenant would ask nicely if we needed water and tell us to, "Watch out for that New Orleans sun."

Prior to leaving Metairie Manor, we took another break from

the searing star and unwound back in the dinning hall. There was an old jukebox near the entrance. One of the nuns took advantage and played an old tune. She shared a brisk dance with one of the volunteers. I was sitting next to an older African American woman by the name of Pamela while the dancing took place. We discussed what it was like to go out and have fun when she was younger.

"Oh, you see what they're doing right there?" she asked, pointing to the dancing members of my group. "I think, I think, they call that the swing now. But when I was younger it was the jitterbug. Those were the steps, my dear. It would always getcha movin'."

"Did you dance a lot?"

"Oh yes, years ago. But I'm older now. I like to see ya'll young-ins have some fun. Sadly, we don't get to see that too much 'round these parts anymore. But watching ya'll brings me back to those exciting nights. Boy, when I was younger, my papa wasn't a fan of us younger girls going out to dance or anything like that. But my mama, she taught me a coupla dances...secretly. My sister and I, well, we would practice late at night in our room. Get our steps down just right and just have fun. Ah, to be young again...thank God for ya'll. Cuz some of these folks forgot what it was like to be young. It's nice to see people coming 'round these parts. Ya'll give us good memories, something this city needs."

Passionately Unfurnished

Day two in New Orleans. I woke up in my bedroom facedown on the black T-shirt I was using as a pillow. The T-shirt was positioned on top of my deflating air mattress bed. My neck was aching. My back twitching with discomfort. My memories filled with recollections of the previous date. I could still hear the sounds of furniture breaking. Racket symbolizing a broken yesterday. It was time to prepare for a recovered today.

When our carpool had arrived again at the Nazareth Inn, the laid-back maintenance man said that we would be working on the "second building." This "second building" was a structure indistinguishable from the first one. This building was the Nazareth II. It was roughly ten feet from number one. Separated only by the scalding asphalt.

Geared up, we entered the cluttered Nazareth II and stood in a foul lobby waiting for the sluggish elevator. Whilst waiting, we had the opportunity to meet a slim, jovial, African-American repairman. He popped into the squalid lobby with a beaming smile and a gust of exhilaration, "Oh my, look at all these fine young folks we got here. Ya'll gonna be helping us out today?" The group responded with excitement.

"That's good, that's good. How ya'll like it here in New Orleans?"

One of the sisters cheerfully answered, "Our time here has been so pleasant thus far. Everyone we have met has been incredibly nice."

"Yes! I'm so glad to hear you say that, you don't understand," the ebullient man replied. "There's lotta people out there in the world that believe only in what they see on that there news, or read in them papers. But not me, ya'll. My name is Jimmy, but my friends call me Butch, so ya'll call me Butch," he said, getting a kindhearted response from our cluster. "The only time I hear the name Jimmy is when them bill collectors come-a-knockin' HA! But no, really. If ya'll see me on the television, ya'll know Butch ain't there doing nothin' negative. Butch is doin' somethin' nice and helpful. Just like most of us folk out here.

"Everybody think we're robbing and stealing just cuz they seen that on the news. That's only cuz that's all them reporters and news programs show. Everybody in the world think this city is a damned circus show. All them programs just wanted to watch and point their fingers, and they treated us like animals. But that ain't the truth. There's good, hardworking people in this city. Ya'll gotta remember that."

The slothful elevator finally arrived and Butch waved us off. The crammed elevator ride was silent. Full of anticipation. *What would we see? What would we learn?* My group got to our first room and it was atrocious. Judged against the rooms we worked on the day before, it was ten times worse. Shocked from the accumulation of rubble I mumbled, "Jesus Christ."

The nun leading our group and standing behind me whispered, "You're right. We should pray." And that's what we did.

We prayed. Then we cleaned. We tossed. We emptied. And we moved on to the next rooms.

The last room we cleared out consisted of a tear-jerking sight. On a tiny, portable stand, a small table used to eat meals in front of the television, sat a bowl filled with putrid milk and rotten cereal. Most of the cereal stuck the sides of the bowl. To the left of the bowl laid a vital newspaper with the date—August 29, 2005. It became evident to us that the occupant of that room was having breakfast when the hurricane came roaring in, forcing the inhabitant to leave their breakfast and dash off to who knows where.

The cereal bowl was as a reminder of that grisly day. It was in that house for two years. In shadowy seclusion, waiting to contribute reminders. I stood there attempting to envision the fright and the exigency coursing its way through that occupant's body. The bewilderment alone must have been too much to handle.

When we completed our work for that day, I went back and walked through the rooms we cleaned. They looked habitable. But they still had a sentiment of despondency. They were now emotionally vacant. I knew what was once there, what had happened due to Katrina, what became of the resident's possessions. And now, I saw the bareness that lingered.

Car Ride of Knowledge
Painting New Pictures
The Reemergence of Reality

It was my last day in the steamy city of New Orleans. For our final day, the group went to an apartment complex called the Christopher Inn. We helped the residents by painting their chipped apartment doors.

Prior to our arrival at Christopher Inn, the volunteer group had the opportunity to drive all around New Orleans. The sights were explained to us by Ann, our articulate, blonde-haired tour guide. I was fortunate to be in the same car with Ann given that she had to use a walkie-talkie to communicate with the volunteers in the other vehicles. I'm sure they must have missed a few things due to static.

We drove for a while, cruising through various streets, getting the chance to observe brilliantly built structures through the windows of the cramped mini-van. We saw the uniqueness of the eloquently bizarre trees, swooping into the jungle-like front yards of the New Orleans-style homes. After we passed one aged building that used to be a homeless shelter, and another house where Ann Rice once lived, we began the doubly compelling aspect of the tour.

Repeatedly bouncing around as we drove over an assortment of potholes, we finally crossed over the Inner Harbor Navigation Canal, or as the locals call it: "The Industrial Canal." The Industrial Canal passes through the "ninth ward." From what I saw, the ninth ward was the most ragged and impaired site in all of New Orleans. The houses that once stood in the ninth ward were all gone, all smashed and hauled away when the storm broke those levees.

After our wheels finally stopped their rotation, we got out of our vehicles, and placed our feet onto the soil of the annihilated lower ninth ward. The lower ninth was a neighborhood formerly filled with houses, but two years after Katrina, it was no more than vacant land covered with dense, overgrown grass and weeds. The only trace of enduring construction was a row of three shattered houses. The stunned volunteer group started walking the rutted dirt-path toward the houses. But a camouflage-clad Caucasian security guard, sporting a hunting knife on his right hip and wearing a green Desert Boonie Hat, instantly cut us off.

"Whoa, whoa, whoa people… This here part is closed off, sorry?"

"We just wanted to look at those houses," a volunteer said.

"Well, them destroyed houses are just part of a movie set. We're setting up for a new Hollywood movie. Although that's what the real houses looked like after Katrina, those houses are not actually real. We just re-created 'em," he told us. "My name is Paul, I know everything there is to know 'bout this area, I can help ya'll out if ya'll got some questions."

Paul spoke to us a little about the movie, how long he had lived in New Orleans, and how much he loved the city. He was a very knowledgeable person when it came to the history of New Orleans. Paul went on to tell us about a past hurricane called the, "Billion-Dollar Betsy," which caused havoc over forty years ago and was "just as dreadful as Katrina." "Hurricane Betsy," Paul stated in his New Orleans nature, "oh boy, a lot of people have forgotten about that little beast." Paul then pulled out an assortment of graph charts and pictures from one of the pockets of his green jacket. "You see the similarities between Betsy and Katrina?" he inquired, pointing to the graphs.

"I'd never heard of Hurricane Betsy," one of the nuns declared.

"Oh yeah, it was the 1960s version of Katrina. Water levels so high some people drowned in their attics. This area all around here, the ninth ward was completely done for. It was the same as you see it now, *this* is exactly the way it was forty years ago, thanks to Betsy..."

Paul then ended his train of thought by saying, "That's what's so painful for us as a city, ya know, the reoccurrence. I mean, you want to see people live freely, choose what's best for them and their children, and rebuild their lives. But at the same time, I think we *have to* draw a line on the reconstruction of the ninth ward. 1965, Hurricane Betsy. 2005, Hurricane Katrina. What's to say that devastation won't happen again in another forty years? Or maybe even sooner. We don't know. And I don't think we're provided enough resources to plan." After a long pause he whispered out his last sentence before saying goodbye, "Whatever the plan is for the future of this city, I think it is disappointingly hopeless to rebuild the ninth ward."

Ann told us about her New Orleans upbringing while driving out of the ninth ward. "That's why it's still so hard to deal with this catastrophe, even though it's already been two years. The pain never goes away. You have those memories of how it once was and then you see how it now is." She then began expressing her thoughts on George W. Bush, "The reaction time was just despicable. I do not understand how a tragedy in a country that you are supposed to be the leader of takes you four days to start making decisions. It was probably because it didn't deal with his immediate family. I mean, Mr. Bush did send a good portion of money for hurricane victim's relief, but the problem is once the money gets here it goes directly to the heads of the local government, and truthfully, the people only see small scraps of that money. The people with the power are just fine, but those that embody New Orleans are really struggling"

More driving ensued while Ann spoke ill on the New Orleans Mayor, Ray Nagin. She especially disliked a speech he delivered on January 16, 2006, "Mayor Nagin's speech on rebuilding New Orleans as a 'Chocolate City' was hurtful and distasteful. Phrases like that can only harm and delay the future of an encouraged union for people. We don't need a man in the public eye promoting disconnection. Even before Katrina, Mr. Nagin was sparking racial separation. But he was just reelected for five more years. But I, along with many people I've spoke to, are almost certain that his organization paid lump sums of money to bring people in to vote for him. I really can't see how the people would want him back in office."

Still guiding us around New Orleans, Ann leisurely steered past a senior complex called St. Rita's Nursing Home, in the St. Bernard Parish. This nursing home was the building where thirty-four people had drowned in Katrina's torrent waters. The nasty story had received much deliberation while also being bound by vagueness.

Ann sternly informed us on what she had heard on the subject of the awful account, "Essentially, many people died. The water flooded into the building and many older folks and disabled people were stuck with nowhere to go. They couldn't move and they were basically left to drown. I am not too certain about the entire story. I don't know if the caretakers of St. Rita's just ran out and left the residents stranded, but for the sake of humanity, I really hope not.

"The whole event is truly horrible. You really *have* to think about the poor families of these people when it comes to a situation like that. And if it was at all possible for the caretakers to help the immobilized in that nursing home, but they decided not to, well…may God have mercy on their souls." I looked over to one of the sisters sitting in the front passenger seat. Tears dripped from her face.

Following the tour we arrived at the Christopher Inn. We immediately began painting the resident's doors. I was geared up and facedown on the tarnished tiled floor, painting the bottom of a stranger's doorframe. I was only halfway done with the frame before the apartment door opened and made me drop the paint-brush on the filthy tile.

A tall, slender Caucasian man emerged with a cigarette hanging from the right corner of his mouth. He stared at me while I was down by his feet. He was a bearded man with faded tattoos on his forearms. He wore khaki shorts and an almost completely unbuttoned Hawaiian shirt. He finally removed the stick from his lips and spoke in a cool raspy tone, "Hey there, guy. How's that floor treatin' ya?"

"Actually, it's a drag on the nuts."

He took another pull off his cigarette while telling me his name was Ken. He invited me inside. His apartment was filled with artwork and made me feel at home. He offered me a smoke. Then, letting out a lengthy groan, Ken took a seat on his shredded couch and began telling me about a "rock 'n' roll club" he used to own.

"It was a hopping place, brother. I owned and ran the joint in the French Quarter, probably, uhhhh, thirty-three years ago, I think. It was like a second home for me. I had to quit the biz because the wife didn't like me comin' in at four in the mornin' stinkin' drunk." Ken paused to stare at the ceiling of his apartment. He reminiscently laughed for a few seconds. His laughing stopped, a couple of calm puffs of his smoke passed, and his faced twisted to solemn ogling before he spoke again, "But she passed away and now I miss her, man. I even miss those damn arguments we'd have when I'd come home wasted. I used to have a nice two-story set-up...beautiful livin'. But when she passed, brother, I moved to this apartment.

"There wasn't no reason for me to have a house after she passed...no matter how many people I put inside that fuckin' thing...it just felt empty. Plus, what don't hurt is the fact that my boys live across the lake," he said pointing out his apartment window. "Ya man, I guess you could say...I guess I could say that I don't mind it to much here. I got jazz clubs close by and family even closer."

Not wanting to miss a beat, I started talking about Charlie Parker and Duke Ellington. It must have made him excited because he got up off his couch and started showing me his own works of art. Paintings he called his "Jazz Art." They were images of jazz musicians wailing away on the sax.

"You should take this to New York, man, try your luck on the street. People would buy this up in a second," I told him.

With a grin on his face he told me, "Maybe someday, brother, maybe someday. But for right now, I like where I'm at. I love New Orleans. Even when I'm lonely, I'm never lonely ya dig? I always got someone to talk to. I can always turn the corner and find somebody. The pride of this city is what keeps me moving. That's why I hope the people forced to split have the opportunity to come on back. I think it's impossible to forget where you come from, and with a city like this, you not only have the opportunity to relive, but you can also create new and improved memories."

Once we finished at the Christopher Inn, the volunteer group had a farewell dinner in the French Quarter. Then we walked and enjoyed the sights. I had a nice laugh while walking down Bourbon Street. Strolling with a New Orleans' rum concoction called the "Hurricane," I witnessed a man with an electronic signboard strapped to his chest, flaunting messages that read, "You choose abortion—You burn in hell. You gamble—You burn in hell. Premarital sex—You Burn in hell." It was funny because a pair of stripper's legs were hanging from a window no more than two feet behind the man with the motorized message. Contradiction at its finest. But that's what makes New Orleans "The most unique city." It's never hard to find individualism.

The end came to the short week in New Orleans. It was time to take off. Get back between soaring wings and return to the Garden State. Once again, I was the volunteer sitting next to strangers. But this time I was in the middle seat with a middle-aged man to my right, who was already sleeping prior to take-off, and to my left was a pleasant-looking, elderly woman in an graceful yellow dress. A silk headband was wrapped around her head to keep her short, gray hair out of her shimmering blue eyes.

By the time the plane took flight, I learned that this radiant woman, whose name was Susan, was down in New Orleans delivering care to her sister who was living in a nursing home. Throughout our conversation, Susan had a glow of dynamism beaming from her body. As she spoke, sunlight came piercing through the small window from the opposite side of the airplane. The beams gave her the appearance of a seraph.

"This is beautiful," Susan said, gliding her soft fingertips over the tattoo on my right forearm.

"Oh, thank you. It's the prayer of eternal rest for my father and stepfather."

I realized it was the first time that I did not feel uncomfortable giving details on the ink. The tattoo had always been just for me, and, due to my own peculiar rationale, I have persistently avoided any moment of explanation. Yet, while leaving New Orleans and flying the passive winds, sitting next to the virtuous Susan, I felt unusual.

I felt at ease explaining all the ink on my body. Realization suddenly hit me. My capability to reveal had come from my time in New Orleans. Being with an assemblage of volunteers so comfortable with themselves, being with the people of New Orleans who were massively confident about the future, made me feel safe for the first time in a long time. I felt as if I was flying with divine assistance, with the beaming sun steering my course.

Susan asked me questions, inquiries I had heard before. But this time my answers were in a different light. A glow of naturalness. Answering Susan's questions about my tattoos, I was no longer repeating myself. I was contentedly reliving. I also embraced the opportunity to talk about my time in New Orleans. Susan listened to every word.

I talked and talked, and she listened. And, unexpectedly, as I was still carrying away with what I had seen in the Crescent City, we were already landing in Newark. After I realized how much my frame of mind had completely 180'ed, before we went on our separate ways, Susan tenderly shook my hand and asked me what I wanted to do with my life.

"I want to tell encouraging stories."

The Bass Goes Boom
Written in New Orleans

The Bass Goes Boom,
The Bass Goes, Boom.
Ready the tombs. They faced continual gloom; fatal doom.
Yet, The Bass Goes Boom.

Vivacious faces are now traceless; they can't breathe, the city is
*   purple.*
The devil's breeze carried debris, nothing left normal.
Yet, The Bass Goes Boom.

Tears rain on vacant soil they once called home.
Entire families washed into the sinister unknown.
Yet, The Bass Goes Boom.

The mind shakes; this is far from great when one thinks of gracious
*   fate.*
Apartments forlornly laced, old papers in cold empty space trace
*   Katrina's date.*
Yet, The Bass Goes Boom.

Now there is a multitude of attitudes, hatred and vile styles.
But fusion prevails, giving the victims their motivating smiles.
And even though their disheartening tears could fill the emptiest
*   pond,*
The PEOPLE, their LIVES, the SAINTS have switched gears and
*   will go marching on.*
The Bass Goes Boom.

VOLUME 3

WASHINGTON D.C.

Prologue

Washington D.C. epitomizes the act of vitality. When I arrived there I noticed that the population was definitely on the grind, nearly comparable to New York City. Normally, Washington D.C. has a resident population of over 588,000 people. But due to the commuters and the heavy demand of labor, that number increases to over one million during the workweek.

A large number of citizens living in the bordering states of Virginia and Maryland voyage into the District for work. Before the first of my three trips into the nation's capital, I read that many businesses such as law firms, independent contractors, nonprofit organizations, lobbying firms, national associations of labor, and other professional groups have their headquarters in or in close proximity to D.C. in order to be close to the federal government. With that said, never one to shun, I wanted to go to the District myself and learn just how many people were truly yearning for income.

I got in touch with an old friend of mine, Whiskey Maze. He was living in D.C. and I needed a place to stay. Generously, he offered me some temporary lodging and "a couch to relax."

That's all I needed.

Back in the Saddle, Back on the Road
Lessons from the Observer
Understanding Protest

The trip from Central New Jersey to D.C. is about three and a half hours. My friend Todd agreed to take the trip with me. Peculiar thoughts frequently occur when one is alone for a long period. So I appreciated the company.

I scooped Todd up and we hit the road. The somewhat lengthy drive was filled with a variety of emotions, all expressed at full speed. In the first hour, we had a nice mixture of calm chatter while Muddy Waters motivated from my speakers. Cigarette smoke hurriedly vanished out the driver's side window. When we reached the second hour of driving, Ol' Dirty Bastard was experimenting with melodies.

Everything felt different yet familiar.

There is something special about that guiding roadway. It ignites. I believe the road releases all timidity while also allowing excitement to emerge. But long trips can also create juvenile delirium. So when we drove into D.C., I began howling and honking like a madman. At nothing in particular mind you. I just felt it was the appropriate thing to do.

We advanced down the road and blazed through a traffic light, which was on the brink of turning red and where three African-American men stood dressed in awfully old and threadbare clothes. They were standing side by side selling roses. The noise inside the car abruptly died down.

"What happens if they don't sell those roses?" Todd asked with his dark eyebrows arched, exhibiting the sincerity of his indispensable inquiry.

"I don't know…I guess they can't eat for the day."

My remark made me think about Antoine. The Blood I met in East Orange. I wondered if he was still selling phones or doing odd jobs to get food.

Whiskey Maze's two-story apartment was a great scene. Partially because I was out of my car and pleased to see a sofa. But also because his apartment was eye-catching. Hardwood floors. Two television sets situated abreast. Behind the televisions was a large sliding door that led out to the balcony. When I walked out onto the terrace I knew I was in a unique location.

The highway was directly below. Speeding cars eating up the road. Past the highway was the Watergate Hotel. Switching positions and gazing to my left, I stared at the Kennedy Center, a place where grand talent is expressed. I knew when the next morning rolled around, I'd be at the ideal scene to question and embark on the process of learning.

When the morning arrived, it delivered punishment. I woke with up a hangover of mega proportions. Whiskey Maze, being the great host that he is, brought Todd and I out to a local bar called Porter's. Along with the morning hangover, the night of drinking also delivered weird dreams involving stolen hats and shady lawyers defending me in court.

Hazy. That is all I recall about my dreams. Perhaps my penalty for stealing hats in my Dream World was several pokes to my right eye, because, when I woke up on the living room couch, my eye was throbbing. Every time I blinked the pain would establish at my iris and steadily shoot back to my central retina vein. No reason to stop myself though. All I needed that day was one working eye. Thankfully, both of my feet were still functioning.

I marched. It was 12:00 p.m. when I started walking down 23rd street. I was on target for the monuments. Chipper college students all dressed in athletic attire surrounded me. Some were making their stroll more active by flipping water bottles in the air. Others were passing soccer balls back and forth, eager about their upcoming matches. For some reason, most of the people kept repeating the phrase, "The early bird gets the worm."

It could have been a crack on me, seeing as my physical appearance rebutted their phrase. I was dressed in the same wrinkled clothes that I wore the night before. I reeked of debauchery. I was moving at such a sluggish pace. I kept telling myself to move faster. My mind knew how to transport the message to my legs but those ligaments refused to cooperate.

The soccer players moved on and I continued with my tempo. Before long, a fresh crowd drew near, most of them communicating by use of a wide array of languages. And then, just like the others, they vanished. No problem. It felt good to value my slow pace.

My first stop was the Lincoln Memorial. Numerous tourists jammed the area, all snapping pictures, hoping to get the shot they can everlastingly remember. As I continued to peruse with my one good eye, I noticed many young couples in love at the monument that day. All of the affectionate duos had identical routines. The boyfriend would take a picture of the girlfriend. Then switch positions. Then grab a lonely soul, like myself, to snap a picture of them together.

I jogged up the steps with my own camera in hand. Once I reached the summit, I was smacked with astonishment. There he was—Lincoln sitting proudly in his enshrined pose.

Lincoln's powerful energy forced me to take a step back. By doing so, I unintentionally bumped into a gangling Caucasian man. His serious features were partially covered by his neatly groomed white beard, which intermingled with his blindingly white hair. I lifted my foot from his and apologized.

"Watch it, guy. I'm taking pictures," the man said while using his thumbs to massage his camera.

"I see that," I fired back. "What're you taking pictures for?"

The man looked like Colonel Sanders. He let out a hefty and heinous groan and walked away without saying a word. He proceeded to snap photographs a few feet away from me. I was a bit puzzled. Was my question too difficult to counter? I wondered if his photography was robotic. Was he there simply because it was *The* Lincoln Memorial? Is the aura of a person, place, or thing all that one requires to take photos?

I looked around at the various sightseers. I wondered if they too were *just taking pictures*. I wondered if the people were there for the quest of knowledge or to fill up their photo album.

After several minutes of people watching, a couple in their mid-thirties asked me to take their picture in front of Lincoln. The husband, Jerry, a tall man who spoke with the studious voice of a professor, told me that they were from Connecticut. He then explained to me how the camera worked. I pretended to listen.

In actuality, my focus was yet again on Colonel Sanders. He had made his way back into my view. He didn't see me though. He was taking pictures of his feet in odd positions.

After Jerry was done tutoring me, he took two steps back to his wife, Alison, and they tenderly embraced with a heartfelt hug. I snapped the photo, handed the camera back to Jerry, and asked the pair what made them want to come to the Lincoln Memorial.

Jerry kissed Alison on her head and gave a fine answer: "Well, we don't claim to be history buffs, but we came to this monument, to D.C., to start understanding what we don't know. That's what it's all about: trying to learn something new everyday, especially about the people around you. And when it comes to the past, there is no better place for this country's history than D.C."

I left the Lincoln Memorial and strolled down a paved walkway with the reflecting pool of Constitutional Gardens to my left and soccer fields filled with brisk players to my right. I felt like I belonged in that moment: in the midst of activity and tranquility. I made my way to the World War II memorial, one large, carved, integrated loop. This National Memorial is relatively new. It opened to the public in April of 2004.

I paced around the memorial twice, reading engraved quotes that stemmed from the battles. At the World War II memorial, there are fifty-six stone pillars, all seventeen feet in height. The names of all North American states are carved into the pillars, as well as the District of Columbia and the Commonwealth of the Philippines, Puerto Rico, Guam, American Samoa, and the U.S. Virgin Islands.

All of these words, these names, these places, these symbols are cemented into history. Joined for any observer to gaze upon and admire.

I moved on to Capitol Hill.

On the lawn of the U.S. Capitol stood a cluster of ten protestors. They were all holding signs. They were an anti-circumcision group. The first protestor I spoke with was Jeff Brown. He was an older man with a gray ponytail down to the middle of his back. His gray, unkempt beard covered most of his face. He was a very soft-spoken man with little to say. All he told me was the natives of Africa brought circumcision to North America.

He said they used it as a form of torturing females in Africa. And, even though the U.S. government banned it for females, he believed the politicians are immoral for allowing it for males. Jeff then told me if I wanted to know more about the subject then I should "talk to Benjamin Lewis. He's been protesting the torture that is circumcision for fifteen years. He knows his stuff." Jeff pointed me in the right direction and I went to go see the guardian of surplus skin.

Benjamin was much more thunderous. Much more frightening. Prior to grabbing his attention, I heard him loudly announcing to anyone listening that, "circumcision not only links but is also the direct cause of terrorism around the world. It is also the reason behind the U.S., Jewish, and Muslim homicidal and suicidal tendencies."

I eventually got Benjamin's attention and he turned in my direction with a wide beam, exhibiting chipped teeth. His eyes were piercing and his glasses, barely hanging onto his nose, seemed like they were going to fall off his face at any moment. He held a sign with the words "Circumcision Causes Brain Damage" printed in big red letters. I asked him about his sign and he wailed, "It's true! It's a scientific fact! Male circumcision is just like female circumcision...it is nothing but mutilation. But for some reason the *government* doesn't see it that way."

"Why do you think the government doesn't see it that way?"

"It's a money thing. Who do you think gets paid to do the operations? This all goes back to the 19th Century. Doctors would remove foreskin and that removal would cause sickness later on down the road for the children, in other parts of their body, and those *same* children would have to go back to the *same* doctors to get treated. It's all a money operation."

"But it's not force-fed in this country. The physicians have to get consent."

"Ah, that consent issue is what most people believe. But there is an epidemic in this country called PFFR, which stands for Premature, Forcible, Foreskin Retraction. It's when the doctors remove the young boy's foreskin without consulting the parents. Also, for the parents that give permission, they need to realize that circumcision *is* a *subliminal* force-fed notion." Benjamin said this while pointing his sign in the direction of a young woman taunting him. "Since the government isn't talking about the repercussions of this mutilation, the people who are circumcising their boys do not know what they are doing to their children."

"What are the repercussions?"

"Deception, brain damage, and war are three major consequences."

"But what about the people who say male circumcision helps to prevent HIV infections?" I asked.

"Lies. All lies by the doctors and the people that they're in business with."

My last question was going to be about the medical use of foreskin after it's removed. But I didn't get the chance to ask. A group of people in there twenties cut me off. They came up next to me and started hassling Benjamin. The spokesperson for foreskin attempted to go into his spiel, but they did not want to pay attention. They simply shouted and walked away.

I stepped back and watched as this incident repeatedly occurred with others. Some people walked past Benjamin laughing at him. Others went up to him and revealed their variation in opinion. When I saw the latter, I noticed the pain in my right eye had vanished. In the past, people have told me, "If something exists, people will complain." Detectably, that statement has always been declared with negative connotations. But as I stood back and watched people protest the anti-circumcision protestors, I began to feel like it was a fine exercise.

People should not expect others to bite their tongues just because their views are dissimilar. Sure, sometimes people's views are far out in left field. But that is the beauty of one's mind. As a child, I was always encouraged to be creative and question as much as possible. As you grow up, those questions sometimes form into protest, which I believe is a good thing if you proclaim your views in a respectful method.

The act of protesting is sticking up for what you believe in. But one cannot begin to do that until they truly learn about their subject. The best part about the establishment of knowledge is that anyone can lay the first brick on their own, assemble independent ideas, and go on building from there. In good time, the structure could be immense. That is if you listen to others instead of mock without reason.

Class is in Session
Gotta Support the Team
Don't Bear False Witness Against Your Neighbor

Back at Whiskey Maze's spot. Ready for round two of my D.C. journey. It has been about two weeks since I was last here. There are some alterations. His apartment is completely different. It is vacant. Whiskey Maze has been living in D.C. and going to George Washington University since we both graduated high school. He has been grinding it out in the nation's capital for the past five years, and now it's time for him to move out and start working in Manhattan.

He is moving on. The only items still in the D.C. apartment are his bed, his TV, a Playstation III, and the living room couch, which will serve as my slumber-spot for the next few days.

When I woke up the morning after I arrived, I started walking around the capital. My attention was grabbed when I became the onlooker of a roaring, energized faction. While heading toward the White House, my concentration was taken elsewhere on the corner of 21st street Northwest.

It wasn't the unwavering bellows bouncing off the buildings that captured my attention. Nor was it the large assemblage facing some unoccupied building. No. It was an enormous inflatable rat perched on the hatchback of a Dodge truck. The rat's ruby eyes peered into the building's windows, toward desertion.

Working in New York City, I have seen my fair share of hot-aired rats placed in the presence of office buildings. Accordingly, I knew that below the crimson eyes of that rubber rat, down on the street level, was a group of union workers on strike, strug-gling against what they felt was industrial disproportion.

In terms of a mass refusal of labor, union workers striking in Washington D.C. is like nothing I've ever witnessed anywhere else. As expected, it was a large group of employees rallying in circles in front of a building...but that was only the first layer.

This collection of strikers, a group largely comprised of African-Americans and mixed with a couple of Caucasian and Hispanic folks, were marching to the beat of their own drum. Literally. One of the repudiating laborers was sitting on the front steps of the building with each hand clutching a drumstick. He used a round, plastic container to perform a drumbeat that put a match to the fire and supported the strikers in their enthused movements.

Sitting alongside the drummer was a woman with long, dark dreadlocks. She was dressed in baggy garments and used the whistle firmly positioned in her mouth. *Drumbeat, drumbeat, whistle, whistle. Drumbeat, drumbeat, drumbeat, loooong whistle.* All of these instrumental tactics fueled the movement.

The head of the strikers was an African-American man wearing gray shorts to match his loose-fitting gray top. He was a hefty man. When he put his vocal self-expression on pause to dance, his upper body was a second behind his legs. Everything about this man was big. Particularly his desire to be heard. This man's voice roused the dynamism of the protestors.

There was no monotone ranting and raving during the strike. Definitely no mutters. The leader of the chants would not let that happen. When it was time to sing, you better believe those chants exemplified a balls-to-the-wall battle cry, a rallying call you could hear from more than a few blocks away. Every time a heartfelt lyric left the striker's body, the obvious target was some corporation. "All they do is cheat and steal!"

There was an elderly man who broke away from the protesting circle. This provided me the prospect of a one-on-one. He walked about ten feet down the street and away from his group. Yet, he remained a spokesperson for the strikers by attempting to converse with others about his strife. He wasn't getting many people to listen. That is until I advanced. I approached and became aware of the large yellow sign covering his chest. The sign said that the company his union worked for did not pay area standard wages and benefits. "What company is that?" I asked the older gentleman.

"Tricon Construction Incorporated," the man said as he patted down his sweaty brow. "That company is treating each and everyone of us like modern-day slaves. Everything you hear from us today is true."

I heard the bloc chanting, "They took our money and we want it back!"

The older gentlemen introduced himself as Albert. I asked him how Tricon had stole money from their laborers. "Well, they're not only stealing our money," Albert said in a poised tone, "they're stealing our livelihood as well." He lightly dabbed his forehead once more with a blue bandana and proceeded: "Tricon pays only seven to eleven dollars an hour, and only the cream of the blue-collar crop get eleven. We're hard workers. Many hours and much effort go into our manual labor, and for what? *Seven dollars an hour?*" Another spectator walked past us and Albert grabbed the sides of his sign and pushed outward as if to say, "Read this! You must *feel* our pain"

Albert turned back to me and continued to express his mentality, "Tell me, how can a respectable man, with the price of everyday goods so high, make it in this world today with such a small income? The companies are supposed to take care of us. We're the ones who are working hard for them. But all they do is make it hard for us to survive.

"It isn't *only* the wages," Albert continued. "Tricon isn't covering our insurance. And they are screwing us with the taxes. We are the ones who are right in this situation. We'd have to be foolish not to speak up and strike. We might be struggling but that doesn't make us stupid. And this is all for a CVS. That's what they want to put in this vacant building. All of this, all of this shouting, all of us getting screwed is because they *need* another

CVS. What makes it worse; there's already a CVS right around the corner.

"It's important to know that we're not doing this outta greed. I mean look at us. That fact is simple to see. We are all adults. Most of us workers got children to feed. That's what's most important to us. And Tricon and our economy makes it real hard for us to provide for our children with seven dollars an hour. So that's why we're striking. To put food in the mouths of our babies and to set the ways for future workers like us, making sure they don't get screwed."

Albert excused himself and rejoined his group. I wished him well and walked across the street. While watching the strikers from across the street I could also see two women in their early twenties walking in my direction. They were looking at the strikers as well.

When they were right in front of me, one of the women portentously said to the other, "This is all so stupid. It doesn't make any sense. They *need* to go to college." They laughed to themselves. And then, they were gone. They vanished as fast as they came. But that one hollow announcement still lingered. "They *need* to go to college."

To me, when one goes to college one generally goes to pursue education, societal betterment, cultural wakefulness, and perhaps become part of a unified group. I truly believe that people seek out these fundamentals because they wish to gain an enhanced tomorrow. Furthermore, as I watched the strikers fighting for *their* better next day, I had to laugh at that woman's rash statement. Even if she did not *see it*, I realized we were all standing on the campus of the striker's unconventional university. Whether that woman could understand it or not, class was definitely in session.

While wandering down Pennsylvania Avenue, the street the White House sits on, I passed scores of merchandise stands. All of them were selling T-shirts, pins and hats flaunting John McCain and Barack Obama's cheery mugs. I could not walk two feet without having my memory jogged of the presidential race.

The whole scene reminded me of a professional wrestling event. I felt like I was in the moments before a big championship match. I was just waiting for a wrestling ring full of steel chairs to pop up out of nowhere and a frenzied man to scream, "Let's get it on!"

The presidential election is so overtly puffed up. It has become a focal ingredient to nationwide glitziness. The one guarantee is that somebody will make money out of this affair. It most likely will not be somebody who needs it. Those T-shirts that are parading the presidential candidates might as well be sports jerseys. It is all about choosing sides. When you bring the element of *team* into big business, everything changes.

The twisted thing about it is that the squad rarely ever alters. We usually get the same ideas, the same promises, the same politics, but we get a new captain every four or eight years, so it gives the impression of modification. The gloomiest detail about this team concept involves the fact that it's unyielding. Once settled on their side, most people will never glance at the other line-up. It's what I call the "I *have to* support my team mentality."

In politics, people become so addicted and emotionally involved in *their candidate*, so overinvolved that they refuse to listen to the other team's plans and curse at the other team's captain. They swear by the fact that the leader of the other squad is using nothing more than shady strategy. When that happens, the entire league suffers and our idea of an intact nation ceases to exist.

We endure the madness because the fans of the opposite side, whatever side that may be, become easily distracted. We all quarrel over how many lies the other team stands for. And we become sidetracked while forgetting that *every member* of the political lineup uses countless ruses. To me, it is distressing to know that a synonym for the word "political" is "taking sides." Have we attached such long blinders to the sides of our heads that we *must* turn down, ridicule, and discount the words of others just because they possess different feelings?

At first glance, I was somewhat unimpressed with the White House. As I held on to the black steel gates that fenced in the White House, separated *us* from *them*, I stared at the legendary structure and experienced a sense of banality.

From where I was standing, surrounded by day-trippers chatting at full volume and gleefully snapping photographs, encircled by collections of street cops keeping to themselves, the White House seemed like a humdrum creature skulking back into a shadowy corner, sheltered from unanimity. I felt somber while looking at the White House.

The White House—ranked second on the American Institute of Architects's "List of America's Favorite Architecture,"—looked like it had been woefully humiliated. I was in the presence of a reprimanded child.

The sounds of a roaring bunch grabbed my concentration.

I spun my body around to investigate the noise. There stood a collection of youthful tourists bordering one very tiny lady. This very tiny lady was stationed on a sidewalk in Lafayette Square, directly across the street from the White House, waving her furrowed hands in the air and chatting with the inquisitive visitors in front of her "stand of peace."

I made my way across the street and walked up to where the action was happening. When I first arrived, I couldn't hear what the very tiny woman was saying. I was blocked off by a large collection of elementary students, all wearing green backpacks. There were so many people gathered around I couldn't even read what the very tiny lady's peace-stand signs declared.

Moving around in the crowd was a couple of older people. One man and one woman. Those adults were wearing green backpacks as well. I pegged them as the children's chaperones. So I tapped the woman on her shoulder and asked what was going on. She looked my tattooed arms up and down and spoke just a touch over a whisper. "I'm the children's chaperone," she said, "and we are all part of the Educational Travel Services."

"What's that?" I asked.

"It's an educational organization that comes together to teach the children out of the classroom," she perfunctorily replied.

"Well, that's nice. You bring the kids out here to get a little schooling?"

"Ya," the woman rapidly fired back. "We want the kids to see and experience things in the outside world. And this woman over here," she said pointing to the very tiny lady, who was still gesturing her puckered hands while speaking to the children, "certainly seems like an experience."

The male chaperone called out that is was time for the students to get going. They adeptly assembled like regimented miniature soldiers and marched through Lafayette Park. In a flash, the very tiny lady and her display were all alone. I stood about fifteen feet away from the "stand of peace." Time to move forward. I strolled over to the very tiny lady who was absorbedly ogling the White House.

As I walked closer to the very tiny lady, the signs and pictures plastered on both sides of her sidewalk stand were becoming more distinct. The first image to catch my eye was a fabricated picture of Vice-President Dick Cheney behind prison bars. Next to that depiction was President George W. Bush tagged as a terrorist.

The very tiny lady was organizing her personal effects and trimly stacking copies of Dwight D. Eisenhower's, *Reflections on War and Peace.*

"May I have a copy of this, ma'am?"

"Of course," she said in a Spanish intonation, pointing to a passage in Eisenhower's written account, which read:

People in the long run are going to do more to promote peace than our government… One of these days government had better get out of their way and let them have it…

"This is the only solution," the very tiny lady said, still pointing at Eisenhower's notes. She then introduced herself as Concepcion Picciotto: "The president's neighbor." Ms. Picciotto was a soft-spoken woman dressed in clothing worn to shreds. Her mouth contained only a few teeth. She told me she had been living on the streets and in front of the White House since 1980. "In fact, I used to have my stand setup right on the sidewalk in front of the White House. But in 1984, President Regan had his people push me back to this sidewalk in front of the park, along with many other protestors. That's just the government's way to keep control over everything. In their minds, it is necessary to control every little detail.

"Years ago they even made us limit the height of our protest signs. I know what they are doing though. From the eighties to the present day, the government is trying to hush the outside voices. They really think we have nothing important to say. They are trying to discourage us by shoving us around, pushing us further away, trying to make us leave. But I have a duty and I will not leave. They will not silence me. They may ignore me, but I am here to prove that free speech is still alive. When I first came here, I left my job to seek justice, and as my days went on, I really found my role in life, which is the quest to ban all nuclear weapons."

"That's your main goal?" I asked. "That's what you want the most? You want all nuclear weapons banned?"

"Absolutely. I am in the quest of peace and righteousness," Concepcion responded without any vacillation, adjusting a pin on her shirt that read: 'Bush Lies.' "I *know* if we stop the production of nuclear weapons, and the creators of genocide, we can use all of that money to get rid of poverty, instead of murdering the people."

"Your mission is not easy."

"Nothing important ever is," Concepcion responded while a stern-looking man walked past her stand shaking his head in displeasure. "But this is my calling. So I am fully dedicated. Sure, there is some harassment out here. Sometimes from the other homeless people, who may want to get physical. Sometimes from people who really do not like my message. I have been physically assaulted before, but all of that will never add up to my goal, the number-one priority, which is the banning of global extermination."

People began to gather around Concepcion's peace stand. I could sense that she wanted to get her message out to the others, so I put my notebook back into my bag and prepared to leave. But before I did, I asked her what she thought about the approaching presidential election. She scratched her face, which characterized a person that lived on the streets for nearly thirty years, and answered in her unruffled pitch, "We have to remember that the governments do not stand for the people. They represent the corporations. If this country has the chance to vote for one of his or her own humans, if we reverse what we have now and a real person, one of us, one with feelings, becomes the leader, we may have some hope. We need a true person on our side. One that remembers that God did not design the planet with borders. If people realize that, they can also realize that we can longer leave people behind."

The Quest for the Forgotten Tribute

Whiskey Maze had moved out of D.C. I needed a place to stay so I could get my last day with the District. I made a couple of calls and got a place to stay at my Aunt Dar's house in the bordering state of Virginia. She was living in another house in Iowa and let me stay at the Virginia house alone.

The morning after sleeping in the living room of my Aunt's house, I left Middletown, Virginia and drove for about an hour into D.C. I wanted to visit a monument I had never heard of before my research. A monument I had not seen during my past two D.C. trips. The testimonial that was on my radar was the District of Columbia War Memorial, which commemorates the Washingtonians who served in World War I. When I arrived at the monument, I immediately understood why I had never heard of it before.

Prior to arriving, I parked my car on Independence Avenue and began asking people if they could lead me down the right path.

But the only thing I discovered from my inquiries was that the District of Columbia War Memorial was just as much of a mystery to me as it was to them. Even the D.C. parking attendants, who generally know the areas they work in very well, just shrugged in uncertainty when I asked for directions.

After some time, I finally realized I was not going to find what I was looking for by walking around and asking. So I flagged down a cab and had the driver help me find the monument.

The cabbie was enormously pleasant and willing to help, even though he had never heard of the District of Columbia War Memorial either. Even so, he was eager to offer his assistance. The cabbie thought I was in the military since I was sporting my

Army fatigue backpack, so that might have peaked his agreeable nature.

I tried telling him I was not in the service but I don't think he heard me. I attempted to tell him that I was not in the military while we were waiting at a red light, but his concentration was elsewhere as he stared at a carefree child running through open grassland, flying a kite with her father.

Still gazing at the child, he spoke such a simple yet wonderful statement. "Look at that child," he muttered. "She's got a happy life in front of her. I just hope she lives it."

A car honked behind us. The cabbie shifted his foot and we only drove for about another minute until we somehow spotted the target. The only reason I knew what I was looking for was due to a picture I had of the memorial. If it were not for that picture, we probably would have driven right past. It's actually difficult *not* to miss it. From a slight distance, the memorial is virtually swallowed up by dreary vegetation. It is only until one walks the short path from a fractured sidewalk to the monument that they can see it clearly.

When I dwell on Washington D.C., and its grand components, the factors that come to mind are the Lincoln Memorial, the Washington Monument, the WWII Memorial, and various others. However, the one structure that never pops-up is the District of Columbia War Memorial. Moreover, once I laid my eyes on the monument, I understood *why* I had never heard of it.

The location blows, mainly because it's hidden away in the woods. On top of that, the memorial itself does not come close to carrying the magnitude of the monuments I just mentioned. Unsurprisingly, there were no kites in the air.

Before walking up to the District of Columbia War Memorial, I stopped to talk with a man in his mid-thirties. He was a pale Caucasian man dressed in all white. He sat with his legs crossed on the grass about thirty yards away from the monument, drawing in his sketchpad. He was sketching the domed top that sat on the pinnacle of the dismal memorial. Knowing how some artists become when they are distracted for too long, I only interrupted the man, who's name was Tim, to ask one straightforward question: *Why was he drawing this dilapidated monument?*

"Well, I mean," Tim began saying, "I'm just an amateur, but to me, finding art in something is actually not that complicated. And it's no different with this monument. The feelings are right out in the open. I've been searching for a long time to draw a piece that seems to have the sole purpose of demonstrating loneliness. I needed to illustrate a motionless subject that gives off the sad emotion of solitude. And as you can see here, this monument is lonely. I've already sketched the top, the dome, the head, you know, the tip of the iceberg. But before I keep going, I have to dig deeper and hit on the reason for the monument's seclusion."

"Because it's been forgotten," I stated.

"Yeah...but *why?*"

Tim looked intently at the cloudless sky. I could tell that he wanted to be alone with his thoughts. Not wanting to bother him, I left without saying goodbye. I walked to the monument to see for myself just how abandoned that artistic monument truly was.

The District of Columbia War Memorial is the most lackluster, deserted monument in all of Washington D.C. Standing by the memorial, the first thing I saw were the names of the Washingtonians who died in WWI. Many names are carved in the monument's stone.

During my time there, most of the people that approached the memorial were those who took a wrong turn and unintentionally stumbled upon it. There were also a couple of tourists who just made use of the wrecked steps to take the weight off their feet, to relax after a long day of checking out the other, livelier monuments.

Well, there were some that did have trouble resting at the

memorial since it was dreadfully filthy. It looked like it hadn't been cleaned since the day of its creation. A stain from some sort of strawberry drink covered a momentous, engraved quote. If that is not a metaphor for "who gives a fuck about this thing?" then I don't know what is. Clearly, somebody not only dropped the ball on remembering the memorial, but also everything it symbolizes.

In 1931, it was unquestionably a great feat to complete the construction of the monument. But, while I was there, the appearance of that same monument provided nothing more than the showcase of cerebral expunging. That self-induced forgetfulness not only overshadows the completion of its erection, it also overpowers the meaning behind its construction. Just because something has been completed, doesn't mean the work is finished.

Walking away from the District of Columbia War Memorial, I was planning to cut across the JFK Hockey Field and head toward the more impressive World War II Memorial to see the sun again. As I was leaving, a family of four, husband, wife, son, and daughter, were walking past me and toward the monument. I could tell by their facial expressions that they were approaching the unfamiliar.

I continued walking and thought to myself that their expressions were great. They did not hear or know of the monument until they saw it, but they seemed to be walking the path of discovery. I marched another twenty yards or so, and for my own form of valediction, I decided to turn around and give the D.C. War Memorial one last look. But when I turned around, I felt my body slow up and my eyes could only focus on that family of four. I realized I was mistaken as to the family wanting to learn the unknown. By the time it took me to stride those twenty yards, the family of four had walked to the monument, looked it over, and decided to split without delay.

I watched as they left the neglected monument and I felt

disconsolate. They wanted nothing to do with that piece of battered history.

At Roundfire we publish great stories. We lean towards the spiritual and thought-provoking. But whether it's literary or popular, a gentle tale or a pulsating thriller, the connecting theme in all Roundfire fiction titles is that once you pick them up you won't want to put them down.